WHOSE FOOTPRINTS ARE THESE?

A FIELD GUIDE TO IDENTIFYING FOOTPRINTS

ANIMAL BOOK 3rd GRADE
CHILDREN'S ANIMAL BOOKS

Speedy Publishing LLC

40 E. Main St. #1156

Newark, DE 19711

www.speedypublishing.com

Copyright 2017

All Rights reserved. No part of this book may be reproduced or used in any way or form or by any means whether electronic or mechanical, this means that you cannot record or photo-copy any material ideas or tips that are provided in this book.

In this book, we're going to talk about how to identify different animal footprints. So, let's get right to it!

If you were a Native American in the 1400s, you would have been able to tell which animals were traveling in the forests or plains where you lived. You'd be able to tell by the dens they built, and by the markings they may have left on trees. One of the easiest ways you could have discovered which animals were around would have been to identify them by the tracks they left on the muddy ground or in the snow.

Being able to read tracks well would have helped you to survive. If you were hunting the animal, then knowing where it had been traveling, and the direction it was going would have been very helpful. It would also be valuable to be able to identify tracks of dangerous animals that you may have wanted to avoid, such as a large black bear!

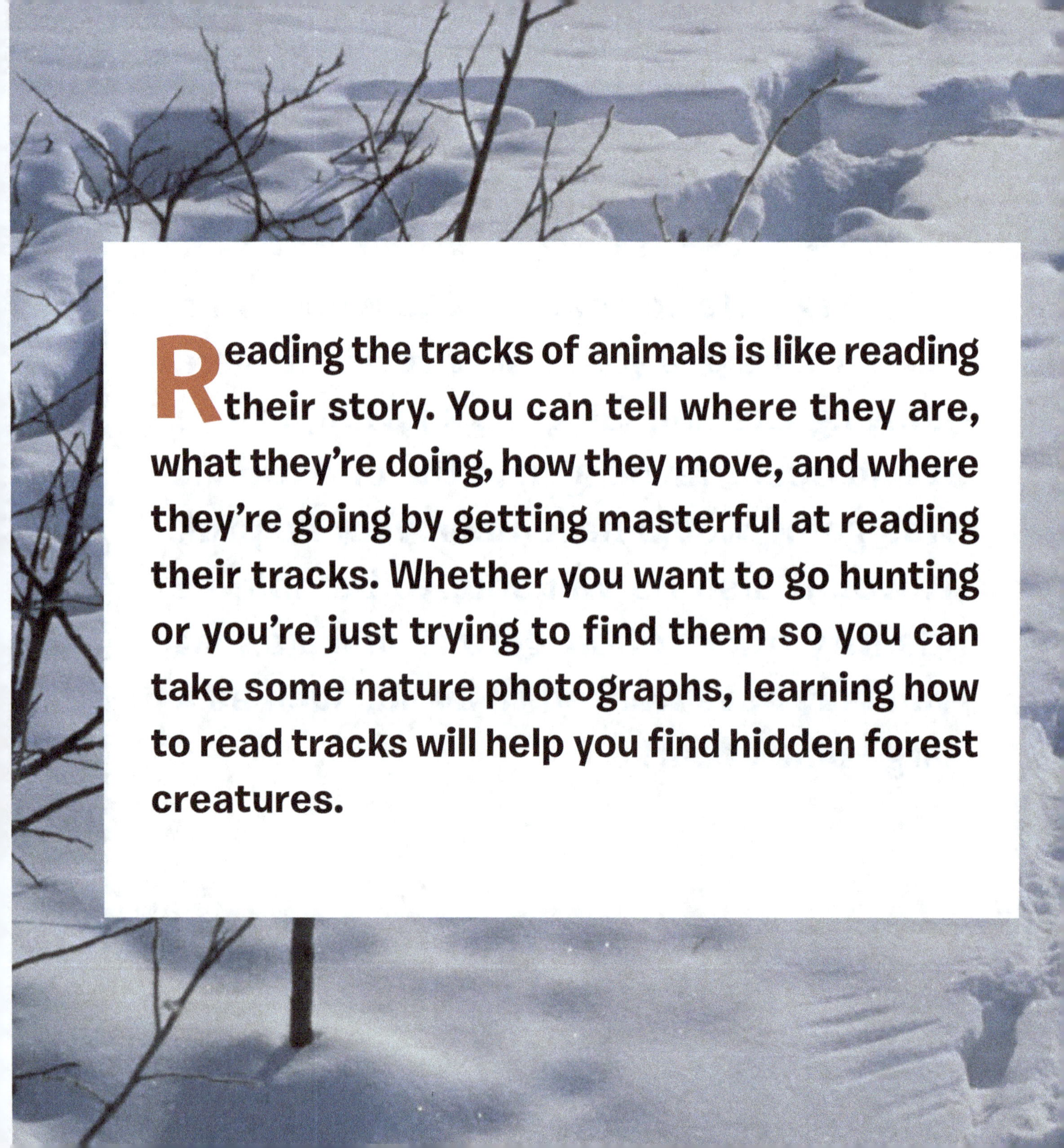

Reading the tracks of animals is like reading their story. You can tell where they are, what they're doing, how they move, and where they're going by getting masterful at reading their tracks. Whether you want to go hunting or you're just trying to find them so you can take some nature photographs, learning how to read tracks will help you find hidden forest creatures.

Before you can start finding animals by looking at their tracks, you'll need to study the tracks so you know how they look and which animal matches with each set of tracks.

BEAVER

Beavers live in the water quite a bit so it might be hard to find a good beaver footprint to study. You can start by looking for the den of wood called a lodge that a beaver constructs on a pond where it's already constructed a dam.

BEAVER

You might even see some evidence of the work beavers do as they gnaw the trunks of trees that they need for their construction work. You might be able to find some tracks in muddy soil around the area where trees have been gnawed.

Another good place to look for beaver tracks are the hills as well as the banks that take you to its waterway. You might be lucky and find a slide. A slide is a muddy section of land that looks worn down and ends in the water. This is where the beaver travels when it wants to go back into the water.

It's a good place to look for tracks. A beaver's front foot is similar to a raccoon's but its back foot is completely different. It has five large toes that have some webbing.

BEAVER FOOTPRINTS

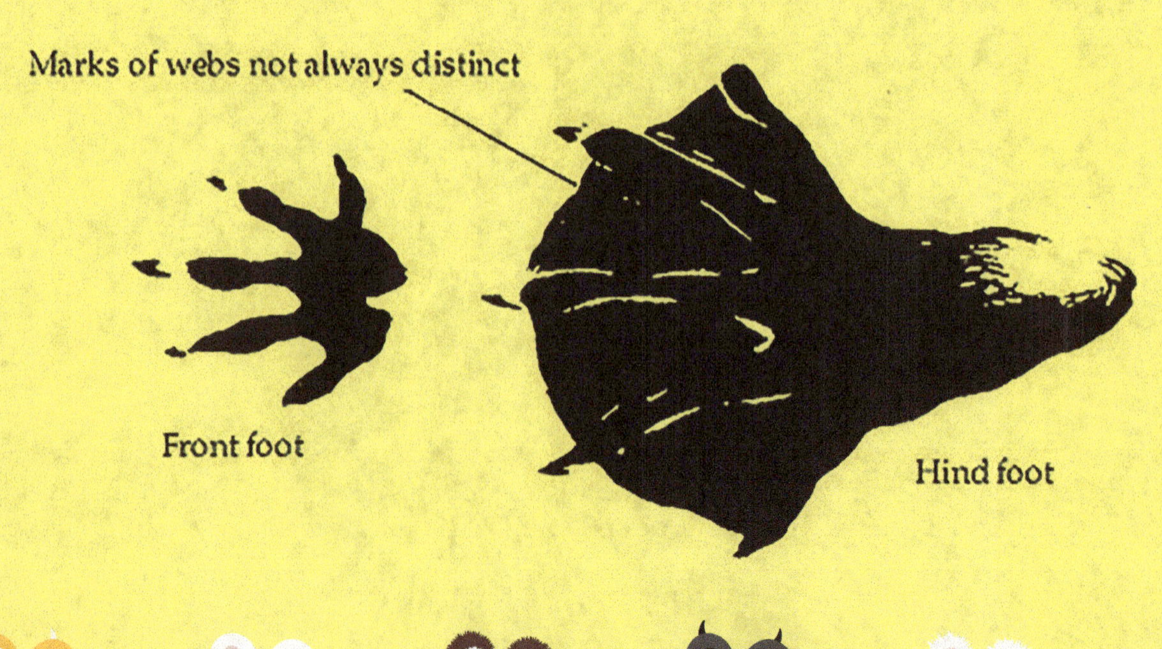

 beaver's front footprints will be about 3 inches long, but its back ones may be 6 or more inches long. Beavers are found throughout most of the United States and Canada.

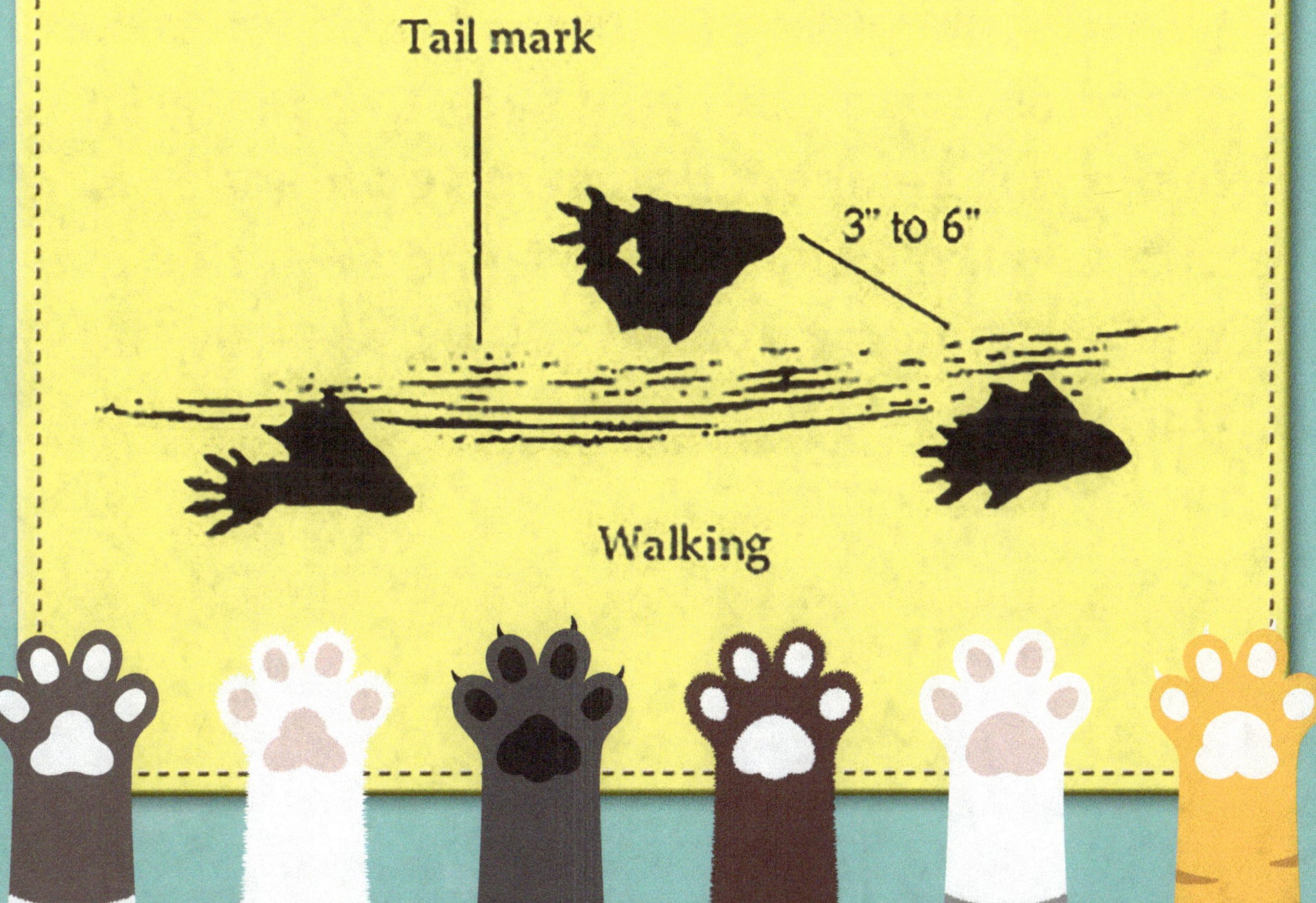

EASTERN COTTONTAIL RABBIT

The Eastern Cottontail rabbit doesn't live in a den underground. Instead, it depends on the forest brush to keep it safe. One footprint might not be enough to help you identify it, but if you're lucky enough to find a series of tracks, you'll be able to tell by the way the rabbit runs.

EASTERN COTTONTAIL RABBIT

It moves with a galloping motion. Its big back feet strike the ground in the front of its two smaller front feet when the rabbit's running. This makes the tracks on the trail look like a pattern of "V"s with the top of the "V" pointing in the direction that the rabbit is traveling.

You'll find similar tracks from other rabbit species such as jackrabbits or snowshoe hares. The Eastern Cottontail has front feet that are 1 inch in length and back feet that are 3 to 4 inches in length. They can be found in the eastern section of the United States, from the state of Texas to the state of North Dakota.

EASTERN COTTONTAIL RABBIT FOOTPRINTS

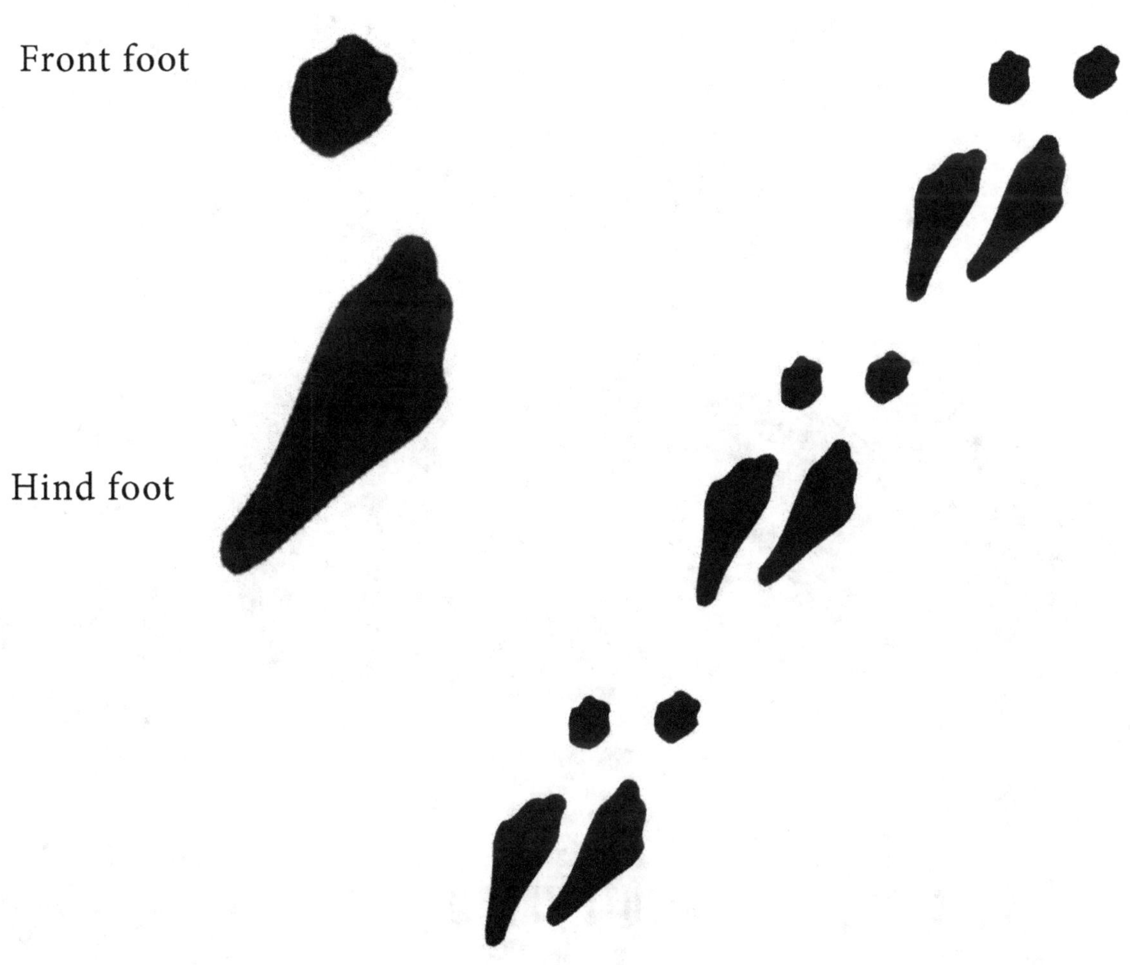

A CUTE RACOON

RACCOON

The raccoon is a nocturnal animal and it's very interesting to track. If you look in the mud of areas that are wet, you will often find long trails they left when they were hunting for food. Both their front footprints and their rear footprints look something like the handprints that humans make. Raccoons have very quick fingers that are useful for catching small fish and opening up shellfish.

Raccoons have five toes on each of their feet. The toes point in a forward direction and are almost parallel to each other. That distinguishing feature will help you figure out that it's a raccoon footprint and not the footprint of an opossum, which has toes that fan out. Raccoons move in a track pattern that is diagonal.

RACOON FOOT PRINTS

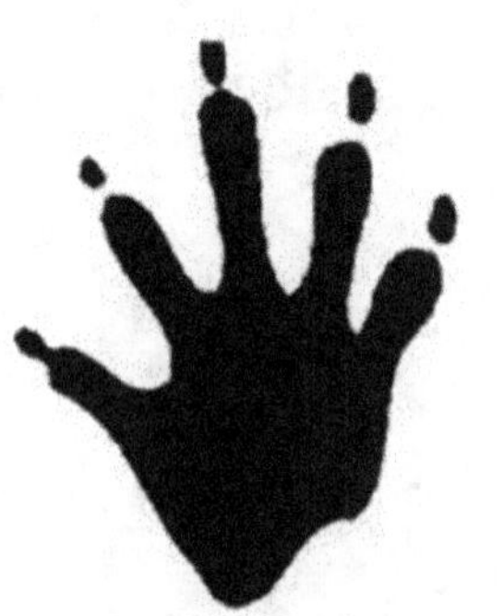

Front foot

Hind foot

RACOON FOOTPRINTS

The rear foot has a longer heel than the front foot does. Their front feet are generally about 2 to 3 inches in length and their rear feet are 3 to 4 inches in length. They can be found in the northern part of Mexico, as well as southern Canada and the continental United States.

OPOSSUM

The opossum is the only marsupial animal that is native to North America, which means the females carry their young in a pouch. Like monkeys, opossums have prehensile tails, and on their back feet they have opposable digits that act like thumbs.

Opossums are nocturnal animals and they hunt at night. If you come across one at night, it might play dead, if it gets scared.

They move very slowly, so they use "playing dead" as a strategy against predators.

In the mud along waterways, their tracks sometimes look like a raccoon's, but if you see the "thumb" digit you'll know it's an opossum. Their front feet are usually about 2 inches in length and the rear feet are usually about 2 to 3 inches in length. They can be found in the eastern part of the United States as well as along the Pacific and Mexican coastlines.

Front foot

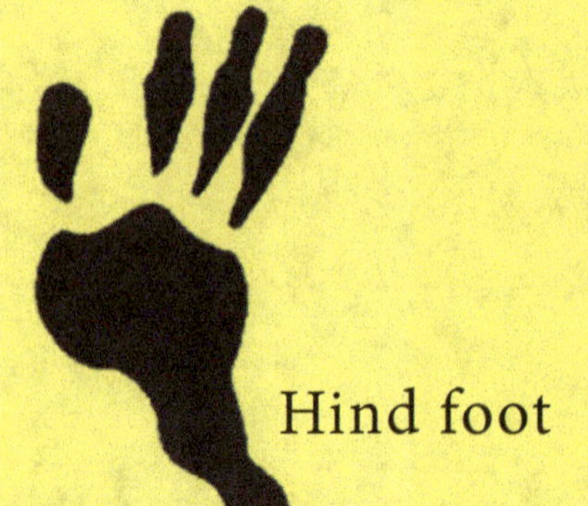

Hind foot

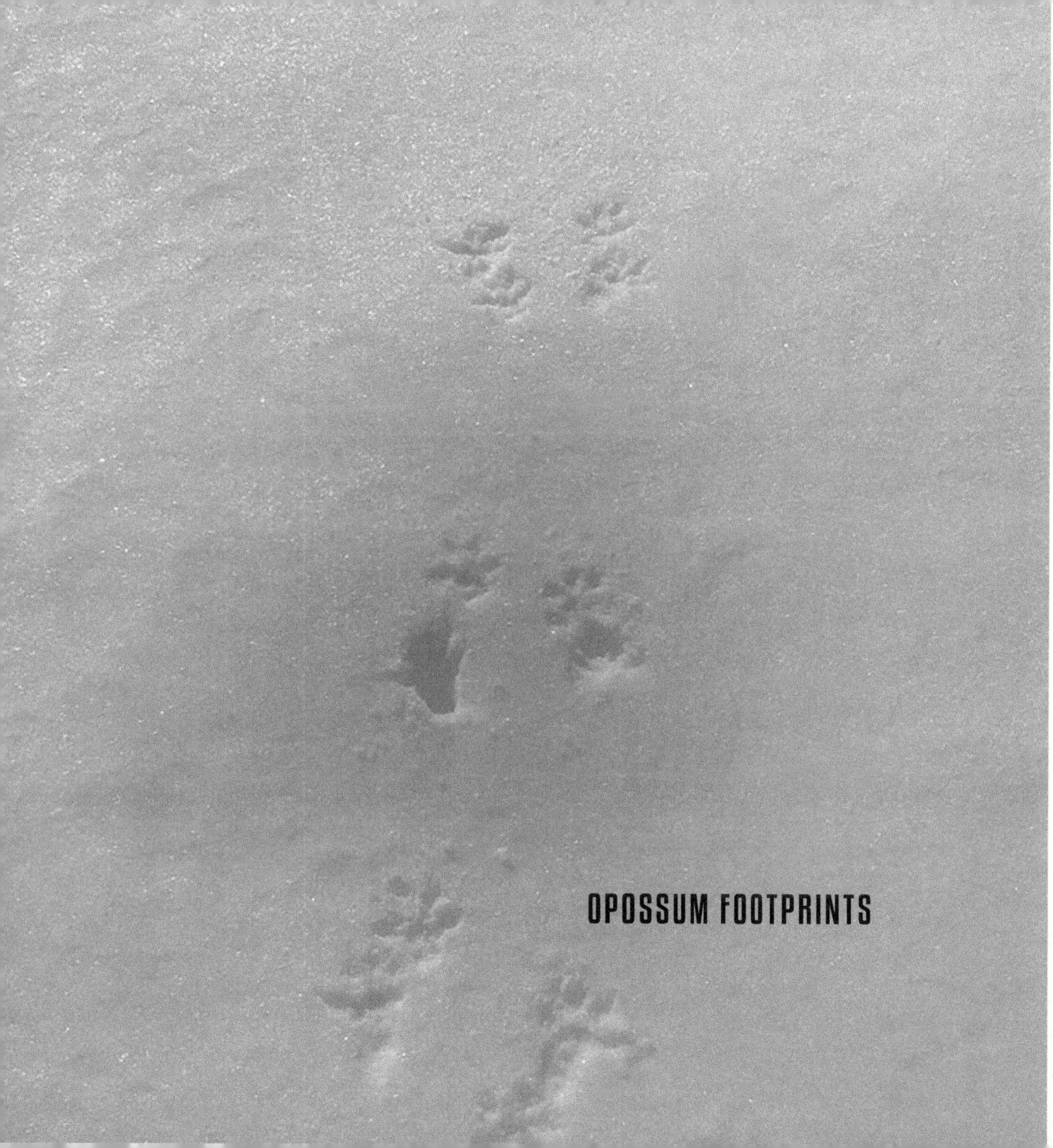

OPOSSUM FOOTPRINTS

COYOTE

COYOTE

Coyotes like woodlands as well as open plains, but they can live almost anywhere. Their tracks look a lot like the tracks of dogs and their droppings do too. If you look at a series of tracks from a dog and compare them to the series of tracks from a coyote, you'll notice that dogs seem to wander, but coyotes move in a straighter line.

It seems like they know where they're going and want to find the quickest way there. Their front feet are a little larger than their back feet and both feet are in the range of 2 to 3 inches in length. They are found in a wide range throughout North America.

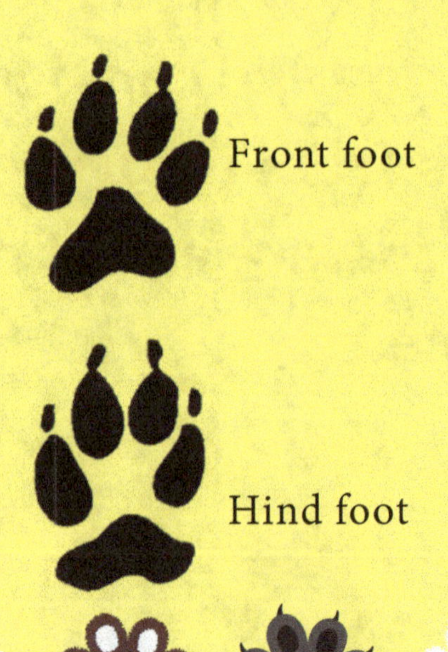

Front foot

Hind foot

RED FOX

RED FOX

The red fox is lean and has a bushy tail that's about half of the length of its body. It's very hard to find the tracks of a red fox. They have very keen senses and remain hidden from predators as well as from humans. They walk diagonally like dogs and deer do.

They usually position their back feet within their front footprints as they walk. They have bouncy steps and very fast feet. Their front feet are a little longer than their back feet with the front feet being about 2 ½ inches in length and the back feet being 2 inches in length.

Front foot

Hind foot

BLACK BEAR

BLACK BEAR

Black bears are dangerous and will kill people if they feel threatened. You don't want to be alone if you are tracking a black bear. They can weigh up to 400 pounds and even though they are usually shy, they can attack with speed and strength.

They have very large tracks and their back feet look something like human footprints. Their front feet are usually about 4 inches in length, but their back feet may be as long as 9 inches. They live in forests, mountainous terrain, and even in swamps in the 48 states as well as Canada.

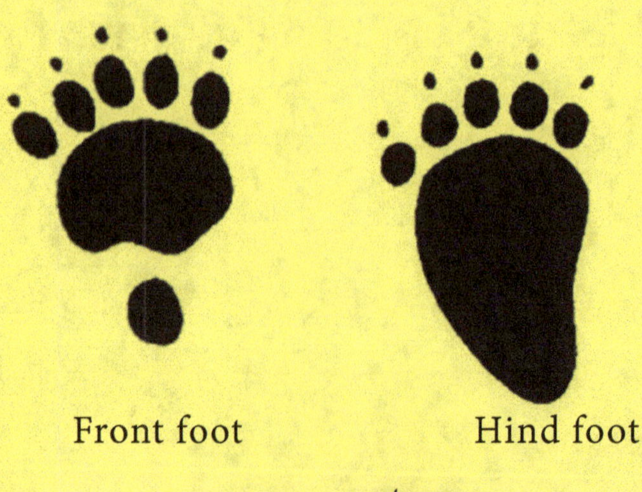

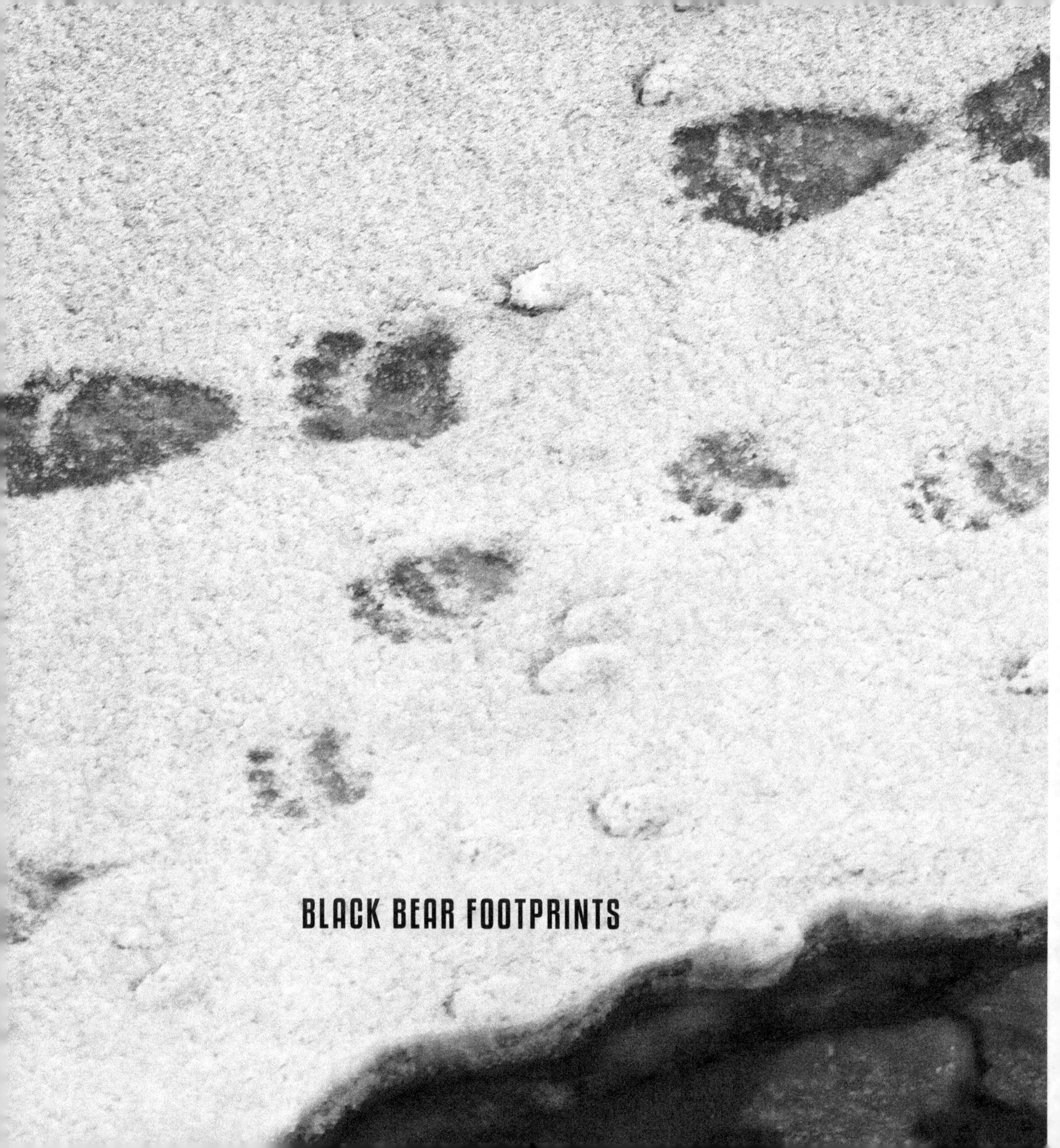
BLACK BEAR FOOTPRINTS

BOBCAT

BOBCAT

Bobcats aren't that much bigger than a regular pet cat, but they have been known to hunt game as large as smaller deer. They walk diagonally like deer and dogs do.

In fact, like foxes, their rear feet land in the front footprints so, when you look at a series of their tracks, it seems like a two-legged animal has been walking instead of a four-legged animal.

Like with most other four-legged animals, their front feet are a little smaller than their back feet. They have small notches in the front of their heel pads. They live in most of the continental United States, except for the Great Plains area.

Front foot

Hind foot

WHITETAIL DEER

Hunters don't have any trouble tracking down whitetail deer to shoot. That's because their tracks are very distinctive looking and heart-shaped. Because deer have sharp hooves, they leave tracks in all different types of soil.

Their footprints are about 2 to 3 inches long and they are found throughout the continental United States, the southern portion of Canada, and northern Mexico.

Front foot

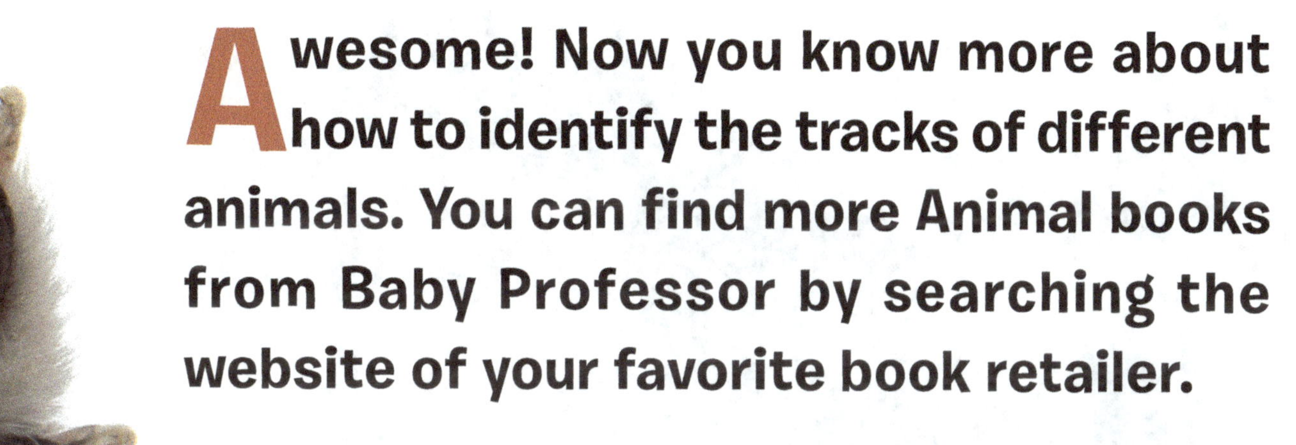

Awesome! Now you know more about how to identify the tracks of different animals. You can find more Animal books from Baby Professor by searching the website of your favorite book retailer.

Visit
BABY PROFESSOR
EDUCATION KIDS
www.BabyProfessorBooks.com
to download Free Baby Professor eBooks
and view our catalog of new and exciting
Children's Books

www.ingramcontent.com/pod-product-compliance
Lightning Source LLC
Chambersburg PA
CBHW080548180726
47999CB00022B/2696